THE NEW SPIRIT

THE NEW SPIRIT

_____

HANK LAZER

Hank Lazer (signature)

Singing Horse Press 2005

The New Spirit © HANK LAZER 2005

Acknowledgments

Several of these poems first appeared in *The Virginia Quarterly Review* (Gregory Orr, Staige Blackford), *Facture* (Paul Naylor, Lindsay Hill), and *Golden Handcuffs* (Lou Rowan), and in the anthologies *POG2* (Tuscon, 2001) and *Another South: Experimental Writing in the South* (ed. Bill Lavender, University of Alabama Press, 2003).

"Prayer" received the Emily Clark Balch Prize 2003 from *The Virginia Quarterly Review*.

Several of these poems also were printed in limited edition broadsides by Oasis Press Broadsides, Lit City Broadsides, and Chax Press.

ISBN 0-935162-30-5
Singing Horse Press
3941 Gaffney Court
San Diego, CA 92130

Singing Horse Press titles are available directly from the publisher at singinghorsepress.com or from Small Press Distribution (800) 869-7553, or at www.spdbooks.org.

Cover image by Grisha Bruskin *Black and Red I, 1991*, Gouachc 23 3/8 x 16 7/8 inches. Courtesy of Mr. Grisha Bruskin and Meyerovich Gallery, San Francisco, CA (www.meyerovich.com).

To Glenn Mott

PRAYER

any one   could be the one   the sudden
stun   you'd waited for
                              arrest again
a rest   against the elements
                                anyone's
unpaginated press
                   persephone personifies   the dying into
dynasty

          how does he hear   this song
among the words   song strung through   the echoing
words   how does he pick a peck   and execute
the singing in his heart   the fire there   a quiet threat
to gods gathered   in that odd margin

                                              *

then they will differ   (& whisper)   if as they do
syllables of willow branch

                          *

tristesse   tristesse

my brothers bless   sold away   sold away
sweet soul   toil by day   sold away   sold away

"so to tell and not to sing it"   the singing   *in* the telling
syllable by syllable   held the echoing way   toil by day
sweet soul   doing as you are told   sold away

tristeza bless   my brother's head

     blues implode
hold him holy   bless my brother   let him live

we think   in fact   we think we hear   so long   so long
the silence couldn't last   long lost lyric   his
body torn apart   *tristeza*   bless my brother's head

the friends of friends   listen at the margins   ink well
speak easy   please the ones   one aims to please
that way danger lies?   a fib   a fibrillation
singing for its own sake   shook in spasm   the arhythmia
of fragmented shudder stutter quick synapse torn orpheus
scattered   no more than a postmodern   did you say
post mortem   period piece   in the authentic rhetoric
the way   this instant   it sposed to be

                                        & i digress

in saying so

                    then again *tristesse*   you settle
too insistently   about my brother's head   bless
the one who risks   adventuring your cause

                                                he
sings it   & he writes it   & he draws it

draws out the thread given to him   threat   threatens
frets   fingers work the frets   plays out the agony
plain song   hydroplaning danger   the rest of us stand
ready to explain

                spell   chant   the god name
a simple exhalation   *yah weh*   *yah weh*
a gust of wind   a single breath   a sacred expiration

no end to what begins
                tristeza
                      let him live

2

to sing then   of happy transience

                                               you move &

move out

               said among elements   not of your making

you in fact   not of your own making

                                           light

upon the instant   given or duration   greater than an
instant

                 time felt as unmeasured   unfolding   you there

placing your order   & waiting   & paying for it

                          *

when this place   like today   a sudden paradise

                                                who
would choose to be elsewhere

                                she pauses   & sits
on a bench   relieved of any obligation to be
beautiful

              song returns in wind   & leaves it too

relieved of preening

                    leeshma   the lyric
                                          each addresses   active
for its own sake   enthusiasm   absent the least self-interest

                              *

too logopoeia

                    please   retune weird word   lurch among lives

say play intent   among productive ardor   order torture fortune

caught on edge   cement elect echo   turn this world

a grave away

                        engrave the way

                                    who says   i

say of time   given to us   singular odd aggregate

we proceed a pace   produce kindred singing   this instant

3

you could tune it   some other way   apparent to
rhythmic conviction   insistent   as you have it   as it
manifests itself   filtered breeze   crisp circle   these sudden elements
sent as breath   said silently   or as actually spoken

what can be heard
                              what can be now attended
to   *hear this*
                    the exact metaphysics
                                        of your historical

moment of listening
                              what does not change   is the
will or   disposition to listen
                                        what does change   is
which rhythms   which combinations of sounds   what music one
in his or her time   is inclined to listen
to
        perhaps *close* listening   but more exactly *beckoned* listening
audition
              summoned from the criss-cross   of your historical circumstance

*

too logopoeia please   stop sermon   cross cut bright elements

fiery filaments shine   *vishnu leeshma corazón*   bright strive honk

talk tongues unclench   to eloquent extension   a pirouette a

parachute for you   a piece of parchment   an arrowhead

a tool for   breaking up compelled incorporation   to speak

of something else   enabled by shaping   breath to turn

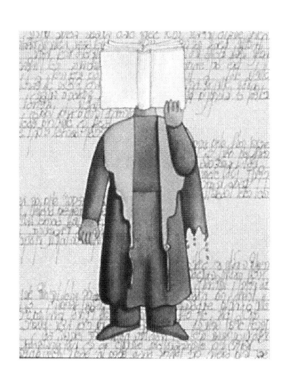

INVOCATION

sum up what you know   you know enough by
now   sing out   what til now   you've kept to yourself
& so declare the daring done

                                        so said the voice   the cadence
in which i heard it
                          breath & ink   fibers so entwined

*

silver   that color   please   i ask you   please   (what place?)

                                                    *

short order   short circuit   shirk it   the shirt you designed the one
your grandmother fanya sewed   on her old treadle machine   an 1880s Singer
that shirt has a priest's collar   why now do you wish to avoid public profession
even as you seek it

                          *

his death   a final step
panting as a dog

                    *

                    your guess as to what   becomes usable

the memorable   not subject to prior manipulation   that scene
his labored breathing   continues to obliterate all others   father

i ask   where are you

                              *

                              harsh quarrel   raised voice
of intimate anger   complaint & disappointment   love love   inextricable

no end to knowing   you know you know   by casting off &
adding on   & every few years or more   some sudden clarification
sinks in   & disappears
                              pleasures of an abiding calm
                                   riding odd cadences of knowing

*

and staring up to stare   face tilted into autumn light   an attitude
of thinking   a surface   upon which to imagine

*

who else   but your young son one day at his sketch pad   to draw
the gateway between being and non-being   human shapes   emerging
& receding

                    each   lives within a different hearing   given to each
that babel   attunes   our differential   thinking / singing   choral
gathering of each genetic specificity

                    difference   difference   difference

                                        the common
denominator
                    in the name of specific rhythmic

                                        in the name of *is*

yakov awoke   changed by the knowing

                                        slipped messages into
oblique code of words   insistence   who's there   it is

*

who that man

                    transmission interrupted

*

if given a life   in the study of words

                                             had been a visitant
had listened   had heard whispers
                                 wind   & intricate perfect

movement   body of leaves   that ornamental pear tree across the street
these fall days   preceding golden
                                        connecting next   to next
to

                    *

one other   who has no job   who has some money   learns
he is an anchor   a light warrior   altering & saving the place where
he lives   receives words & explanations from another who writes down what he
is told from ones on the other side
                                        to say so   in certain ways
gets crazy

                    no known plate tectonics   for the invisible

i hear it   i hear you   this is the medium   here
we are   say it for yourself

                                    *

                                                            call it crocks
of regional shit   trendy mysticism of the under-employed   & so
get busy

                    and what if
                                        amid crocks of digital
cacophony
                    and what if

                                        *

                                        and shed the day
in sleep   arise afresh   in gratitude   in dawn light

"the pulsing life of sound"

5

i am getting   there that new   spirit has such

old roots fragments   unconverted scribbled on   folded over paper

years later learn   these were essential   ones & then

you think you   know what goes   with what &

what might be   of use here   in this country

of domesticated soul   gone smack into   verbally pure practice

*

take the sun for example   or the men &
their bright weaponry   take the gross inequality of lives
privatized ungenerous caring

                                then here   this coffee house   portal
lives relaxed
             pivot
                      or drift
                            into   unimaginable narratives from
which one   much later   rests & reconsiders & recollects
with coffee alone   in some similar lounge   attending then

as now   to a thread of words you've been
putting down
                    & tracking back
                                        a ratcheting tactic   as
gratitude
            for these surprising shifts
                                    & cutbacks
                                                all too
logopoeia   when it becomes a speech   sentences which carry
too adequately   this neutrality of being   with epiphany &
intensity
            tucked in bunk beds   in the guest room

6

in this world   whose ear suzy   o when the

saints i want   to be there   *"plumb crazy core"*

road side desert   to desire wander   in that number

yes money   money first   you can tell that's what
young want & see us as quaint or liars
if we say otherwise
                    gone down   mid sudden mysteries

*

soul upon waters   soul in air   soul goes thinking

scribe sky   soonest mended   shut eyes   embrace shining after-image

verb without complication
                         that state of being
                                air bubbles
rise to surface   & burst   as we are lived

bells toll
        each quarter-hour arrives   departs
                              reaches the surface
against that face
           bursts   bell-toll absorbed   within recurring sky

*

go there   gather as you hear   given circuits in

many languages urge   prayer whisper petition   rise into light

forever ever moved   dance by daily steps to an

altar   in that number   seven times seven years   arrive

at daily gratitude   wake into light   be there [   ]

in that number   love that morning   soul upon waters

TESHUVAH: HEADING SOUTH

this or that   or some such thing   chuck when talking
about a person's capabilities   called it   *wherewithall*   toward the
middle   trane played just ahead of any sense he already understood

*

bless departed ronald johnson who wrote

        anemone mnemonic
          to the least   *ARK* 43
         loomed am

but for absolute bond density   none better   than zukofsky
though ronald could sure as hell slow you down:

          at taps   *ARK* 41
      aft twilit lilac panicle

rafter   beam   arch   colonnade

a cupola fran & ollie show   what's all the hoopla?

chant a rant against the useful dance   thinking of

living   of most instances of a few minutes   honestly

you'd have to say *"what plot?"*

*

when the saints   came final things

or better yet   to very best

      could be consideration will be given

could be we won't wait in line   after all *they* are marching in

could be the doors   could be the hallway   could be the governor will
      unfold his arms & step aside

*

if *flowers say it best*   what exactly is it that flowers say?

lord always then of being

                            homecoming starts with laughs

                                              *

                                                    star

spire   fly forth into   seven elements

fled then into unraveled latitudes   loose   to lucid

cupboard   of summer syllables   foment a cooling firmament

bright hooves break along

                      *

                            furnished according to

                                             *

reveals his glory   early in the morning

                                              *

we are much older   than this would suggest

                                                     so it might

here   become itself   & here (& there)   of adequate complexity

singing as the sign   singing as *dasein*   assign the singing to

our being here & there

                             *

                                  my uncle tells me that neurophysiology
research now shows that in order to see   the eye must move constantly   must
make tiny movements   so that the receptors are not over-saturated by
a single image

                     *

                         we came across frozen archipelagoes

                                                                 *

crossed wolf river   ran along a road of words

listened in the forward movement   of john's blue train

distance is time & miles minutes   crossed hobolochitto creek

linguistic visitant   beloved decadent protectorate   & crossed it again

& then the pearl river

*

tend the flowers   change by season   john the stuttered

phrase accumulated   layered phrasing piling   on the seed

words **rose memory**   **problem chapel crying**   **vibration** *"led on*

by music" "in   *the middle of*   *my life"* necessity

*

finite times to return to this room that measures years

to this room   home of light   loom   permitted to return

finite   as in count your blessings
                                        for each one count
this one

                having found that compact concatenation
                                                percussive sister

                                                        *

a constrained white boy's chant

                                        but damn john
                                        it swings anyway

soul swings to its own dissatisfactions
that   the soul's genetic map   hitched rhythm

                that   & a whole lot more

                (the risk of course being flatness)

                                        *

even with as much as gets forgotten

                                            what is   is unforgettable

much worth knowing   or trying to know

                                              be sure to know

or try to   what love is   & where it exists   as a force
apart from specific persons

                                better yet

                                        whatever it is
                                        have it sing

words on the page   its bodily choreography

the children get older

                which means your own function

                  grows increasingly retrospective
or prospective   & insistent in ways that for others
your vision has no context

                    you chose a set of odd nutrients

            & now   you're precisely where they've

            gotten you

              when the saints

                  in *that* number

                    *

no specific door

or the best words of others

these readings then   *teshuvah*   no other pur

pose but the turning
                    7 x 7 years
                                        the first time through
all seven cycles   then begin again
                            with gratitude
                                    & growing stress
                on retrospect

speak it & sing it

when these had been forbidden

speak it & sing it

resources

begin again

when the senses

as before
the seed phrase   must be adequate

to words in permutations

that death not expected

*

crossed wolf river   ran along a road of words

listened in the forward movement   of john's blue train

distance is time & miles minutes   crossed hobolochitto creek

linguistic visitant   beloved decadent protectorate   & crossed it again

& then the pearl river

8
(in transit)

three little words   *teshuvah* turn toward   you no more

dramatic than this   car moving in   & out of

shadows i love   you & i   have chosen wrong

live with it   three little words   when the saints

when something great   bags & trane   in that number

turn & turn   felt a sharp   turn at 49

*

son at sea lab   cut the squid open   found
the ink sac

        slowly we learn   to work alone
&   with each other

        three little words

                baruch atah

adonai

    love what is

        &   where you are
              take

dictation
    or quit altogether

        user pays connection fee

           drove

south   thinking about this or that   lush southern sound

        *

gateway   i'm here   *shma yisroel adonai*   three word suite

hear o israel   versus nervous be-bop   soul attentive to

its own amusements   play it loud   lord our god

through whatever horn   breathe & shape   heavenly blue legacy

golden fall light   drove me down   the river delta

ghostly sax   tilted back   succession then   when the saints

9

this site gathers together beings   of different times
                                                                         alternate
lives die   & revive here
                                           one by one
                                                                      incite
to thinking singing

                                    it *is* a time machine
                                                                       if
you are so inclined

                                    death   father   we joked about
it quarter century ago   country graveyard   above scrubby apple
orchard
                        this way   back to there   as any day

*

the fog lifts

        allows love for

                what is   *"I*

could not speak before it"

                soon enough   daily chatter

took over

        break it   break it apart   so you

can see it   & rest there

             "it is the

impending I address   *as messenger"*

                  go away   until we

gather nerve to go there

           delicious   how close   first

seeing   feeling   this awakening

                                        entire decades of being   into

Lethe   gone

                    now   i am new   to this age

stirred in   dissolved here   gone into solution   echoic paths

some beings stand guard the troubled heart   art   a

rhythmic charm   magical rant   against loading up the wheelbarrow

instead a load

                    unloaded

                                    enigmatic   as anything   irreducibly real

LEANING TOWARD

said he went   said i went   set to go

they know &   walk across these   silences   they walk

know how   to go over   all the way across

      over frozen archipelagoes   axe heads yes &
          their pictographs

                       when began then
    not mere enumerating   not only toting up who
    has what

          began then singing

               play of thinking

                 *

blessed

say it

      & savor this peninsula
in being

*

"and what Nahmanides seeks for the mourner

is stability

an unextreme attitude   toward extremity"

*

"word itself   has no other foundation"

present in time   of our being together

enter

plenitude

*

to talk about a journey to the interior
         after that language has been dismissed

very funny the way that revelatory sense bubbles up
as gratitude   intensity   vision   as a tangible sense
of significance

                    could be the sight of penguins their
symmetric comic grace   fragile tenacity on the frozen
edge of what we say is livable

                                        *

certain sets among them then

                                        of sounding language ratios

                              *

gratitude also a form of regret   leave-

      taking   mediated by finitude

          soul schooled gradually   into a steadier gratitude

       fin de this because it slides gradually over
       into *that*

           *

he called the language place

the house of being   a dwelling place for time   & the life

of consciousness in it

tenant   in it

subject   to eviction

"there there little one   no reason someone can't get over

that ...."

is

<u>taut</u>

taught

here

*

traction	your face

immediately places me

in time	see	hear

location circulates

soul too has	its own autonomy	& can be felt
taking its own way	a surprise to my thinking	*teshuvah*	soul
turns quietly toward

*

"*the art we address	has passt*

into the mind-store"

*

here   to disappear

this once

an instance   as such

*

where the beam of attention

goes

rhyme itself   but one plausible echo

half off   to damn deaf

soft fall   to falderol

fanya
could inflect a simple *vut* a thousand ways
or   as her son would say   *"seven ways from sunday"*

*

settled among them   & learned their ways of saying   held as well

close to my own   thinking / singing   attuned to invocation

    stuck here   waiting for the word   the next word   the necessary

    word   not of my doing   *"saint"* (as john says it)

    "to raise men from nightmare"

               the tune   a love supreme

         not a known condition

              what *is* that particular love

                 *

to move among   at the threshold   going here &

there by means   of this gateway

                     a span of   rhythmic

joy of knowing   something anything very slowly   old enthusiasms

return   in changed rhetoric

*

enter a tribe of ghosts gone up in smoke   gone all
over the globe   russia lithuania   america   buenos aires
miami brooklyn johanessberg   ghosts smoke circuitous
path for some portion of the absolute text to
reflect upon something of itself   there in the text
owls stoop over   dozing guardians of the
overgrown burrow   sentinels presiding over that sounding
the scattered tribe   gathered about idiosyncratic listening

*

when the saints   when the sepulchre

of my father

a blessing here
& oddly also   a blessing there

i submit the evidence to him

it is for him to say

and when the saints

cacophonous   raucous

soulful stomp   winding through the quarters

grief gone over   into ecstasy

"magnified and sanctified"

*

through red decay   gingko   gone over into golden

*

let through

certain courses   avenues   for feeling   return

acolyte space

a few certain sounds   some rhythmic combination

among the infinite possible   words

beckoning of attention

chasm of   [*that*]   opening inward

precipice   ledge   you dance along

burned into the page

& not consumed

young boy lost in a book   the first in a series   goes to bed
hoping he enters the dreams of it

*

"it is a song of praise

in which the wound   into its river runs"

*

as it is happening   *is*

sung against   or in complicity   with death

*

no doubt   by the time this reaches you

     i will already be

          among the dead

                    books of odd sizes

that place   a road   a café   plain formica tables

metal & red upholstered chairs   green cement floor

fresh mustard greens   pepper sauce   the choral equivalent

     lean into thinking

       "everything i do is leaning   toward

       what we came for"

             *

pain & pleaure in remembering
a handful of dead ones

i see them cross over

*

teshuvah   at any turn   *teshuvah*   possible in any breath

you can then   at some point   feel exact contours of force

the poetry   the life   you will & will not   take part in

that space   & time   do not belong to you

                                        that consciousness migrates

                        & is only for *now* incarnate *this* way

                                                in this

                                                instance

                                                & instrument

                        sounding it out   as you go

Singing Horse Press Titles

Charles Alexander, *Near Or Random Acts*, 2004, $15
Julia Blumenreich, *Meeting Tessie.* 1994, $6.00
Linh Dinh, *Drunkard Boxing.* 1998, $6.00
Norman Fischer, *Success.* 1999, $14.00
Phillip Foss, *The Ideation*, 2004, $15.00
Eli Goldblatt, *Without a Trace.* 2001, $12.50
Karen Kelley, *Her Angel.* 1992, $7.50
Kevin Killian & Leslie Scalapino, *Stone Marmalade.* 1996, $ 9.50
McCreary, Chris & Jenn, *The Effacements / a doctrine of signatures* 2002, $12.50
David Miller, *The Waters of Marah.* 2002, $12.50
Andrew Mossin, *The Epochal Body.* 2004, $15.00
Harryette Mullen, *Muse & Drudge.* 1995, $12.50
Harryette Mullen, *S*PeRM**K*T.* 1992, $8.00
Paul Naylor, *Playing Well With Others*, 2004, $15.00
Gil Ott, *Pact.* 2002, $14.00
Heather Thomas, *Practicing Amnesia.* 2000, $12.50
Rosmarie Waldrop, *Split Infinities.* 1998, $14.00
Lewis Warsh, *Touch of the Whip.* 2001, $14.00

Singing Horse Press books are available online at singinghorsepress.com or through Small Press Distribution—(800) 869-7553 or on the web at www.spdbooks.org.